Simply Science

TECHNOLOGY

Discover Science Through Facts and Fun

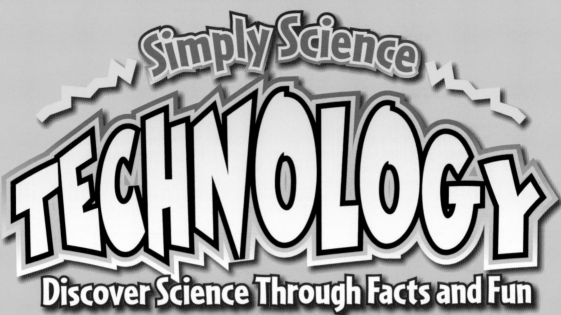

By Gerry Bailey

Science and curriculum consultant:

Debra Voege, M.A., science curriculum resource teacher

Gareth Stevens
Publishing

Please visit our web site at www.garethstevens.com.
For a free catalog describing our list of high-quality books, call 1-800-542-2595 (USA)
or 1-800-387-3178 (Canada). Our fax: 1-877-542-2596

Library of Congress Cataloging-in-Publication Data
Bailey, Gerry.
      Technology / by Gerry Bailey.
           p. cm.—(Simply Science)
      Includes bibliographical references and index.
      ISBN-10: 1-4339-0034-3   ISBN-13: 978-1-4339-0034-1 (lib. bdg.)
      1. Technology—Juvenile literature. I. Title.
T48.B1448   2009
600—dc22   2008027574

This North American edition first published in 2009 by
Gareth Stevens Publishing
A Weekly Reader® Company
1 Reader's Digest Road
Pleasantville, NY 10570-7000 USA

This edition copyright © 2009 by Gareth Stevens, Inc. Original edition copyright © 2007 by
Diverta Publishing Ltd., First published in Great Britain by Diverta Publishing Ltd., London, UK.

Gareth Stevens Executive Managing Editor: Lisa M. Herrington
Gareth Stevens Creative Director: Lisa Donovan
Gareth Stevens Designer: Keith Plechaty
Gareth Stevens Associate Editor: Amanda Hudson
Gareth Stevens Publisher: Keith Garton
Special thanks to Jessica Cohn

Photo Credits: Cover (tc) Andrew Barker/Shutterstock Inc., (bl) David C. Baker/Shutterstock Inc.; p. 5 WizData, Inc./Shutterstock Inc.;
p. 15 David C. Baker/Shutterstock Inc.; p. 16 Phanie/Rex Features; p. 17 Lester Lefkowitz/CORBIS; p. 19 Marek Slusarczyk/
Shutterstock Inc.; p. 21 (t) PA/Topfoto, (b) Phillipe Plailly/SCIENCE PHOTO LIBRARY; p. 25 Andrew Barker/Shutterstock Inc.;
p. 28 Brian Bell/ SCIENCE PHOTO LIBRARY; p. 29 (t) Transport Stock/Rex features, (b) Dean Conger/CORBIS.

Illustrations: Steve Boulter & Q2A Media

Diagrams: Karen Radford

Every effort has been made to trace the copyright holders for the photos used in this book, and the publisher apologizes
in advance for any unintentional omissions. We would be pleased to insert the appropriate acknowledgements in any
subsequent edition of this publication.

Printed in the United States of America

1 2 3 4 5 6 7 8 9 13 12 11 10 09 08

Simply Science
TECHNOLOGY

CONTENTS

What Is Technology?

Can you imagine a world without cell phones, televisions, or computers? Probably not! Yet not long ago these inventions didn't exist. They're the result of scientific discoveries. The science that helped make these, and many more inventions, is called technology.

We use technology to ...
    listen to music ...
find information on the web ...
    watch movies ...
heat a meal in seconds ...
    talk to people in
    countries far away!

Technology has changed the way we communicate.

Technology at Home

Look around you. There are probably gadgets in your home that you use every day without thinking about them. They're all products of technology—even the kitchen toaster!

plasma television

MP3 player

digital camcorder

toaster

microwave oven

washing machine

iron

radio-controlled car

Let's find out about these kinds of technology:

computers
digital signals
microprocessors
cell phones
the Internet
... and lots more!

Fax Machine

The **facsimile machine**, or fax for short, sends a written message or picture through the telephone system.

Inside a fax is a device that is light sensitive. That means it can tell how much light is coming off something, such as a sheet of paper.

If there is an image on the paper, the device will see the light and dark areas on it. The different amounts of light are then changed to an electronic code. The code can be sent to another fax machine.

This receiving fax decodes the message and prints the light and dark areas on another sheet of paper.

1. At first, letters, pictures, and other information had to be sent by mail. It often took a long time for a letter to get to its destination.

2. One inventor made a machine that could transmit a letter by telegraph. It didn't work very well, though. A carrier pigeon would have worked better!

A Letter Sent by Phone

3. A telegraph changes messages into a code of electric pulses. Its code of dashes and dots did not do much good for pictures!

4. Scientists studied ways to change words and pictures into a better electronic code.

5. Telephones were invented. Wire photo machines were put into use. Then scientists wanted to speed things up and send electronic copies by phone.

6. The two machines were linked into one for a new invention: the fax machine. A copier changed the letters into electrical impulses. The impulses were sent down a telephone line to another machine at the other end.

Digits

Modern technology runs on just two numbers, 0 and 1. Just 0 and 1 are all it takes to program a computer. A code that is based on those numbers sends sounds or pictures to your television set.

Two Digits

When we count, we use the **decimal system**. That means we count in tens. We use ten digits, from 0 to 9, to represent numbers. Computers count using a different system—the **binary** system. *Binary means "a thing with two parts."* The digits 0 and 1 make up the binary system. The digits get used in different combinations.

Codes

You don't send your voice over a phone or anything actual through a computer. You translate the sounds of your voice or the colors of a picture into a special code. The code can be made into electric pulses that travel along wires. It can also be made into sound waves that travel from one antenna to another.

Copy Code

Early technology used an **analog** code. *Analog* means "similar to." The sounds or pulses were similar to a voice or to light and dark parts of a picture.

Digital Technology

Today's high-tech machines use the digital system of 0 and 1. This means your voice or a picture get translated into a code using 0 and 1. Your name, for example, ends up as a row of 0s and 1s. Each digit gets expressed as an electric pulse or a sound wave. A zero is like a blank space.

The Computer

A computer is an electronic machine that can record and recall information very quickly.

A task, or job, is put into the computer, usually using a keyboard. A screen, or monitor, shows the information. This is then stored in the computer's memory.

If we linked our brains, we might be able to invent a smaller computer.

An Electronic Brain

1. The first computers in the early 1900s took up a lot of space. They were filled with **vacuum tubes** and other large pieces of equipment. These computers were also very expensive. Only governments and big companies could afford to use them.

2. Things changed in 1947 when the transistor was invented. Computers were still too big to put on top of a desk, though.

A Personal Computer

A personal computer, or PC, can be used by anyone and can fit easily on a desktop. Inside a PC is a tiny microprocessor that operates it. Personal computers use different programs to do different tasks. The most popular programs are word processing programs that help produce all kinds of documents—like this book!

3. They were certainly too big for people to have at home.

4. In 1958, the **silicon chip** was invented. It works like a tiny computer. It can carry an entire **circuit**, crammed into a tiny space. A bigger computer can run on a handful of these chips. Silicon chips made the manufacture of small computers possible.

5. In 1977, Steve Jobs and Steve Wozniak built a more affordable personal computer: the Apple II. Personal computers continue to get cheaper and are one of the most important inventions ever made.

Microprocessors

A microprocessor is a computer chip. In a machine, it is the tiny part that carries out all the instructions in the machine's computer program.

You can find microprocessors in different devices. They are found in calculators, digital watches, and microwave ovens.

Some devices, including large computers, contain more than one microprocessor.

A microprocessor can go wrong when an error known as a "bug," or virus, gets into the program.

How Chips Work

1. The first microprocessors were made for missiles and satellites. They weren't found in everyday gadgets like washing machines. Companies then realized that microprocessors would improve their products.

2. Microprocessors quickly interpret a huge amount of information. The chips are quick and reliable.

3. Microprocessors would help companies build cheaper and more reliable machines. That would save money for people who build or buy the machines.

4. The chips act like a computer's brain. They don't store the data, but they make the data useful!

5. Today, microprocessors get more and more powerful as they get smaller and smaller. The chips are an important part of modern life.

High-Tech Health

Technology helps us in many ways. Doctors and healthcare workers use machines to keep people healthy. Among these machines is one that can scan our brains and another that can track our heartbeats.

CAT Scanner

CAT scanner stands for computerized axial tomographic scanner. It's used for taking pictures of the inside of the body, including the brain. It uses very thin **X-ray** beams and detectors to get this information. It feeds the data into a computer. A CAT scan can tell if your brain is injured or sick in any way.

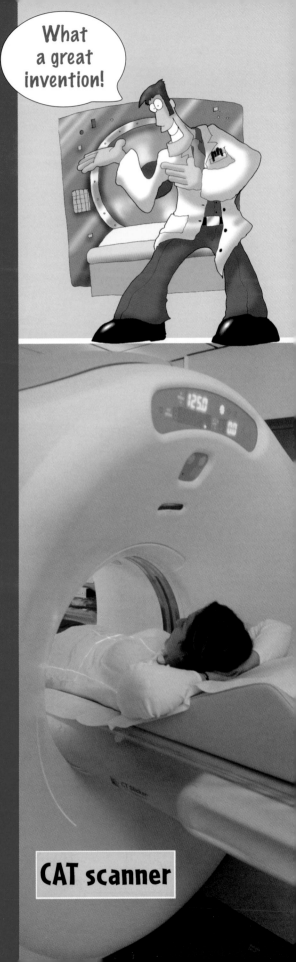

What a great invention!

CAT scanner

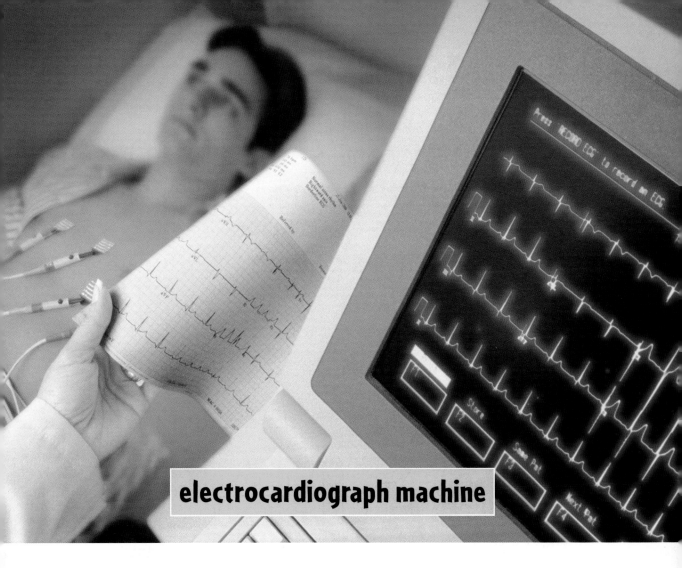

electrocardiograph machine

Electrocardiograph

The electrocardiograph machine records what is happening in your heart. With each heartbeat, tiny **electrical impulses**, or currents, pass through your heart. Doctors measure the pattern of these impulses. Then they can tell when something is not normal.

The electrocardiograph machine records the impulses and prints them out as lines on a graph, known as an **electrocardiogram**, or ECG.

17

Cell Phones

A cellular phone, or cell phone, is a telephone that transmits sound using **radio signals** instead of wires. The signals go to and from large **antennas** placed around the country.

Talking Without Wires

1. Not so long ago, all telephones were connected to wires. This meant, for example, that they were difficult to use on a beach!

2. The first overhead telephone wires were thick. They really spoiled the view. Then special wires were invented that could take many signals at once. After that, not as many wires were needed.

The Network

Cell phone users have a network to make calls. A network has a central exchange. Calls within a cell are collected there. They transmit to other cells via an open-air transmitter.

3. Other inventions came along, such as automatic telephone exchanges, but they didn't make a big difference in how phones worked. Telephones still needed wires.

4. Then people started using radio waves, not wires, to carry telephone messages. Portable phones became possible, though the first ones had to be close to their power source to keep their signal.

5. Then came satellite technology! Huge antennas were built. Each gave out a signal over a small area, or cell. So when a caller moved out of one cell, their call would automatically be taken over by the next one.

Warfare Technology

Technology has often been developed to make better weapons and communication devices for war. Army officers know they must use up-to-the-minute technology to keep ahead of the enemy.

Guided Missile

Guided missiles carry explosive warheads. They are steered from the ground, ships, or aircrafts.

TERCOM

Some guided missiles use a guidance system called TERCOM, which means Terrain Contour Mapping. The system takes pictures of the ground, or terrain, below, at regular times. These pictures are compared to maps on the computer. If they don't match, the missile changes direction until they do.

Troposcatter Modem

This device bounces radio waves off clouds and dust in the atmosphere, without satellites.

A British army artillery unit uses a computer and maps to plan ahead.

Ballistics

Ballistics experts use computers to study what happens when a bullet or missile is fired. They look at how gravity affects the flight of the missile. They study wind resistance. Their aim is to make the missile go as far and as straight as possible.

Compact Discs

A CD, or compact disc, is a round, hard piece of flat plastic. It is coated with a soft metal called aluminium.

CDs are mostly used to store music. They can store more than an hour of sound. The sound is carried in a spiral around the disc. Instead of the grooves that old record albums used to have, CDs use a series of hollows called pits. The flat surfaces in between are called flats.

The spiral of flats and pits is read by a **laser beam** in a CD player. The player turns light into electric signals to produce sound. Many people now use portable music players.

1. Record players, or phonographs, made it possible for people to listen to music in their own homes. The sound was recorded on a cylinder. The sound quality was not great.

Light and Sound

2. Next came the flat disc and gramophone. The first discs were made out of a resin called shellac. Shellac is made by insects.

3. Luckily for the insects, the shellac discs were replaced by vinyl ones. Vinyl is a kind of tough plastic. The sound was stored in grooves cut around the disc.

4. There was still some background noise. To solve the problem, inventors tried laser technology. Laser is a form of light. A beam of laser light can act as a needle. Dents in the disc can take the place of grooves.

5. Each time the laser light beam hits a dent, or pit, different electrical signals are sent out. These are changed into specific sounds, which is what we hear ... as music!

New Horizons

Technology allows us to explore new horizons, such as space and the oceans. Super computers have powered astronauts to the Moon, while submarines explore wrecks and wildlife far below the sea.

Virtual Reality

What if you could go anywhere you wanted to go? It is possible with virtual reality. A computer creates a whole world for you. You can fight dragons or visit the center of Earth or Mars!

Submersibles

Many submersibles are operated by remote control. They use computers and digital cameras. Scientists no longer have to send divers into places that are too dangerous or too deep.

Radio Telescope ▲

A radio telescope collects **radio signals** from space. The radio waves are turned into electrical signals. Their strength and the way they travel is recorded.

A computer can then tell where they came from and what caused them in the first place.

Spectrograph

A spectrograph analyzes light that comes from stars in space. It breaks that light into the colors of the spectrum. The arrangement of the colors tells the contents of the star.

The Web

1. In the 1960s, the U.S. Army wanted to develop a communications system that would survive a major enemy attack.

2. This got the scientists excited. They began to work on a way to make a network of computers that could talk to one another.

They developed a system known as **ARPANET**. It allowed the computer systems of four U.S. universities to communicate with one another.

3. Of course, everyone wanted to join in—to create a SUPER network! It was not enough to connect just four universities.

4. The possibility of one giant network linking small networks across the world was beyond exciting. A huge new supernetwork was built. It is called the Internet.

5. A computer expert called Tim Berners-Lee wrote a software program that allowed sound, pictures, and images to be sent all over the world on the Internet.

Internet

The web, or world wide web, is part of a computer network known as the Internet. It is made up of electronic addresses called web sites.

The web works like a giant encyclopedia. It provides text, sound, pictures, and moving images that bring information to every web user. The web can also be used to create design, audio, and video projects.

Into the Future

We already see some amazing technology around us. What do you think we will be using in the future? Some gadgets give a hint at how things might be.

Universal Communicator

Future mobile phones will be able to translate calls into any foreign language. This would allow people to talk to anyone in the world, in any language!

Head-Mounted Display

An HMD is a head-mounted display. It's like a computer screen that you wear. Today, HMDs are used by pilots to help fly military aircraft. They are also used to create virtual reality environments for games. Perhaps one day you will wear one to watch shows instead of staring at a big, old-fashioned television screen.

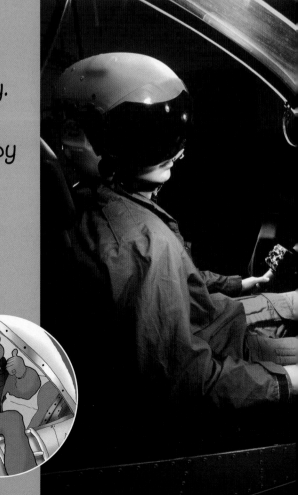

◀ Flying Car

Imagine flying cars with room for two people. You take off from a field near your home and fly where you like. After landing, you take the wing off your vehicle and continue by road—just as if you were traveling by car today.

Jet Pack

A stuntman flew with a jet pack at the opening of the 1984 Los Angeles Olympics. Today's jet packs are heavy, so people can't travel very far with one, but who knows what the future holds?

▼

Force Fields

In science fiction stories, a force field is a barrier of energy that protects a person or a thing from attack.

We now have an electric force field that protects armored vehicles against anti-tank grenades. It can vaporize copper bullets before they are able to pierce the tank's casing. What will be next?

Technology Quiz

1. What network works like a giant encyclopedia?

2. What kind of technology analyzes light from the stars?

3. How is sound produced from a CD?

4. What is a tiny computer chip called?

5. From where can a guided missile be directed?

6. What are cell phone transmitter areas called?

7. What technology is used to look at your brain?

8. Which type of animals were used to help make the first records of sound?

9. What kind of machine uses light-sensitive technology?

10. What could an electrocardiograph be used to check?

1. The world wide web. 2. A spectrograph. 3. A laser reads pits and flats on its surface. 4. A microprocessor. 5. From the ground, a ship, or an aircraft. 6. They're called cells. 7. A CAT scanner. 8. Insects. 9. A fax machine. 10. Your heart.

Glossary

analog: a signal based on a physical change, such as a needle in a groove

antennas: metal rods wired to send and receive electromagnetic waves

ARPANET: the (a)dvanced(r)esearch (p)rojects (n)etwork, the original Internet

ballistics: the science of motion and objects, such as bullets, shot forward

binary: an electronic signal based on two digits, 0 and 1, in order or a series

circuit: the complete or partial path over which an electrical current can flow

decimal system: a number system based on ten numbers, from 0 to 9

electric impulses: sharp, moving electrical waves

electrocardiogram: a graphic that traces the electric forces of a heart beating

facsimile machine: a device (fax) to send a copy of graphics over the phone

guided missiles: vehicles guided to targets by control equipment, not pilots

laser beam: a column of laser light, which has intense waves

microprocessor: a circuit holding a computer's core elements on a chip

radio signals: electromagnetic waves of a certain kind, used for radio

silicon chip: a small crystal made to carry a fully connected circuit

vacuum tubes: devices that changes an electric signal by controlling its movement in an emptied space

X-ray: a high-energy ray of specific measures

Index